ST IVES
THEN & NOW
IN COLOUR

ST IVES ARCHIVE

PITKIN

Pitkin Publishing
Pavilion Books Company Ltd
43 Great Ormond Street
London WC1N 3HZ
www.pavilionbooks.com
Sales and enquiries: 0207 462 1500 / sales@pavilionbooks.com

First published in 2014
Reprinted by Pitkin Publishing   1/19

British Library Cataloguing in Publication Data.
A catalogue record for this book is available from the British Library.

ISBN 978 0 7524 9908 6

Printed and bound by CPI Group (UK) Ltd, Croydon, CR0 4YY

CONTENTS

ACKNOWLEDGEMENTS

We would like to express our appreciation to those who have donated images to the St Ives Archive database: John McWilliams, the Rose Lodge, Jane Geen, the Shore Shelter, David Elsbury, William Thomas, Ross Barnes, David Pearce, St Ives Town Council, Lee Sheldrake, Rachel Opie, the Leach Pottery and the late Keith Lloyd. Special thanks to St Ives Museum for the photos on pages 13, 44, 46, 59, 71. And finally, especial gratitude to Mike Murphy, whose IT expertise we couldn't do without.

ABOUT THE AUTHORS

This publication has been compiled by volunteers of St Ives Archive. They are:

GRETA WILLIAMS. Greta spent many years as manager of St Ives Library. On retirement she fills her time in many ways, first of all as a busy grandmother and great-grandmother, then as an ardent member of St Ives U3A. She is treasurer of St Ives Speech and Drama Festival and also enjoys world travel with her husband. Any time left over is devoted to St Ives Archive. She is happy answering general queries at St Ives Archive and has been known, occasionally, to make tea. Greta is very proud of her Cornish roots.

JOHN MCWILLIAMS. A former primary school teacher in St Ives, John's family had boats for many years and he has always had an interest in local and maritime history. As a teenager he spent a lot of time aboard the visiting Breton fishing boats and sailed to France with them. In 2007 he wrote their story, *A Century of Friendship*. He was made a Bard of the Cornish Gorseth for his research in Cornish maritime history. Like Greta, he is much involved with his four grown-up children.

BARRIE WALKER. A chef who has run a St Ives guest house with his wife for the last twenty-three years, Barrie's introduction to photography came in 1978 with a Pentax ME super film SLR camera. He has been a member of the St Ives Photographic Group for twenty-one years, many as competition secretary. A great deal of his leisure time is spent capturing the Cornish seascape. He has had work accepted in international salons and won awards in the Cornwall Photographic Alliance and the Western Counties. Outside of work and photography Barrie enjoys family life and has great satisfaction from the title of granddad.

INTRODUCTION

Wouldn't it be nice to see the beaches, streets and alleyways of St Ives empty of all visitors in high summer? The town would then show a traditional face to the world, a town that has changed little but whose economy has completely transformed. The seine nets, luggers, fishermen, quarries and mines have been replaced by pleasure craft, bathers, crowded beaches and bustling streets.

But wait, do we really want the town to be devoid of all visitors – those who drive our present economy. Let's look back. In past times, the Downlong streets were busy, they bustled with large families filling the tiny cottages, and spilling out onto the cobbled streets, to chat and gossip, children to play, nets to mend, memories to share. A romantic image, perhaps, but let's not forget, these were really hard times. The mines were closing. Fishing was a dangerous and precarious living. Families lived 'hand to mouth', and our beautiful harbour would have been dirty and smelly. One far-sighted entrepreneur thought he would like to build a hotel close by the harbour, but his ambitions were defeated when he realised that the smell would deter his guests.

This book endeavours to portray, through images, the town as it was and is now. The project has thrown up some interesting anomalies. One is the fact that Downlong now consists mostly of holiday accommodation – and where do the dustbins and recycling bags fit into our wondrous street images? Motor transport does not create the same romantic image as pony and traps.

Geographically our book leads the reader from Porthmeor Beach, through Downlong, around the harbour, along Porthminster Beach, up the Stennack, through Ayr and Penbeagle and on to the mining area.

St Ives is now considered to be a top international holiday destination, and our beaches regularly feature in 'best of' publications, together with our award-winning restaurants – who would want to spend their holidays anywhere else?

The St Ives Archive is located on the first floor of the Parish Rooms in St Andrew's Street, opposite the Parish Church. Opened in 1996 and staffed by volunteers, the Archive is a valuable resource for anyone wishing to obtain historic information about the town. The 'Then' photographs in this book are from the Archive's extensive collection of 20,000 images of the area, taken from the mid-nineteenth century to the present day. The 'Now' photographs have been specifically taken for this publication.

St Ives Archive, Upper Parish Room, St Andrew's Street, St Ives, Cornwall, TR26 1AH. Telephone: 01736 796408

PORTHMEOR PUTTING GREEN

PORTHMEOR PUTTING GREEN, 1940s. Putting at Porthmeor has featured in St Ives holidays probably since the 1930s. In the background, on the left, is the gasworks dating from 1835. The tall red brick retort house, an unlamented eyesore, was built in 1932. On Friday, 28 August 1942 the gasworks was attacked by two German Focke-Wulf aircraft which had just machine-gunned Porthmeor Beach. Many people were picnicking and enjoying the sunshine. The girls at Flawn's factory were outside enjoying their lunch break. Thinking they were Allies, they waved to the pilots. Sadly, Mrs James was killed while returning home with her shopping. Mr Casley Langford and the St Ives Council gasworks staff were congratulated for quickly re-establishing the gas supply.

PUTTING IS STILL enjoyed at Porthmeor but the background has seen many changes. The gasworks has been replaced by the Tate Gallery, centre left. Probably the most famous grave at Barnoon cemetery, right, is that of primitive painter Alfred Wallis, made of tiles by famous potter Bernard Leach. It shows a lighthouse with a man entering the door at the bottom, on his journey to the light at the top. The story of St Ives Tate began with a hugely popular exhibition of St Ives paintings, sculptures and ceramics at London Tate in 1985. A whole train full of Cornish people travelled to London to see the exhibition. This was one of the encouragements for the idea of a gallery of modern art at St Ives. Locals wanted to see our St Ives paintings at home. Enthusiastically supported by St Ives Tate Action Group, the Tate St Ives was opened by Prince Charles on 23 June 1993. The imaginative building was designed by Evans and Shalev and still excites admiration and it is estimated that St Ives Tate welcomes 200,000 visitors annually.

PORTHMEOR BEACH

PORTHMEOR BEACH, 1930s. Until the coming of tourism, Porthmeor was a dumping ground for ashes from the gasworks and the location of one of St Ives' smellier *pig towns*. Here bathing machines (left) and tents are for hire. Monday washing is spread on the north side of the Island with St Nicholas' Chapel at the top. On the right is the chimney of Crysede Silk works where silk was printed to designs by Alec Walker, its founder, and made into the latest fashions. The girls who worked at Crysede were not allowed to talk but they were allowed to sing. Many of them collected remnants from their work which they made up into much-prized garments. Crysede provided very welcome employment in St Ives at a time of industrial depression. But there was no tradition of factory work in West Cornwall and the locals needed training. This part of St Ives later had several factories including Flawns, who supplied John Lewis.

Its workers enjoyed a trip to London to see its products on sale. The wall along the beach on the right was built under the direction of eighteenth-century mayor John Knill to prevent the old town being overwhelmed by windblown sand. Its construction enabled the streets and pilchard cellars of Downlong to develop during the nineteenth century.

PORTHMEOR BEACH'S BATHING machines and tents have been replaced by colourful windbreaks and banners for the popular Surf School. Porthmeor is one of Cornwall's best-known surfing beaches. In the foreground are the RNLI lifeguards' quad bike and jet ski. On the right are Porthmeor Café and the Meadow Flats. Top right are the recently completed Porthmeor Beach Flats. This development will soon include an extension to St Ives Tate Gallery which will provide new gallery space, a collection care suite and new visitor and staff facilities.

THE ISLAND

CAMPING ON THE Island, 1930s. The visitors' and locals' needs co-exist with sheets drying in the foreground and tents and caravans overlooking Porthmeor Beach.
On the left is the Island Cellar, formerly a pilchard works but then used by Crysede Silk. The drying space on the Island was demarcated into sections for washing, *barked* nets and tarred ropes. *Barking* was the process where nets were dipped in hot liquid, made with an eastern bark, locally called *cutch*. The hot bark killed the bacteria from the fish, which would rot the nets, and preserved their fibres. More recently, nets were preserved in creosote known as *pickle*. Tarred ropes were dried on the wall by the Island Meadow. The Downlong housewife would not have enjoyed seeing her washing coated with tar or *pickle*. In the background work has started on building Beach Road and Channel View, known as *Fishermen's Row*. Local families had begun to leave the narrow streets of Downlong and, like the seagulls each evening, to *go to the westward*.

THE VIEW FROM the Island eighty years later. The old studios and net lofts by Porthmeor Beach have been converted into blocks of flats, St Nicholas Court, Barnaloft and Piazza. Porthmeor Studios and Cellars have recently been sensitively restored with a strong emphasis on retaining their original features. Design was by Long and Kentish. The project emphasises the century-old link between the St Ives fishing community and artists. Funding has included support from the Heritage Lottery Fund, English Heritage, the Convergence Programme and European Fisheries Fund. The cellar beneath the property is one of the few remaining Cornish pilchard cellars, complete with concrete tanks where the fish were salted. It retains many original architectural features including the iron pipes and huge wooden beams which support the roof. These were recycled from local tin mines. The studios have been used by eminent St Ives artists including John Park, Hyman Segal, Bryan Pearce, John Emmanuel and Naomi Frears. The building includes the St Ives School of Painting, founded by Leonard Fuller in 1938.

THE ISLAND BATTERY

THE ISLAND BATTERY, *c.*1894. There were six guns on the
Island during the Napoleonic wars until 1815. A new battery of
three cannons was completed in 1859 at a time of concern about
possible war with Napoleon III's France. They were removed in
1894 but the old granite-built battery with its three circular gun
mountings remains. One of them holds the National Coastwatch
station. The National Coastwatch took over visual lookout after
the Coastguard withdrew from this service in 1994. St Ives
Coastwatch began in 1999. During the early twentieth century
the Coastguard lookout had a tall mast which was used to make
flag signals to passing vessels and for hoisting a *north cone* when
a northerly storm was expected. Below the Coastwatch is the
Lamp Rock where a light was lit every night to guide boats into
Porthgwidden, which was a fishing cove in the seventeenth
century. In the background is the ancient St Nicholas Chapel,
destroyed by the War Office in an act of accidental vandalism
in 1904 and rebuilt in 1911.

THE CANNONS HAVE long gone from the Island Battery. On the skyline is St Nicholas' Chapel, one of St Ives' two surviving medieval chapels. The other is St Leonard's Chapel at the top of Smeaton's Pier, which contains a memorial to St Ives fishermen lost at sea. In the sixteenth century the building served as a lighthouse as recorded by Leland, who wrote in 1538, 'There is now at the very point of Pendinas, a chapel of St Nicholas, and a pharos for lighte for shippes sailing by night in these quarters.' In the eighteenth century it was used by Revenue officers to look out for smugglers. The War Office used it as a store and, unaware of its importance, demolished it in 1904. There was an uproar and it was rebuilt by local shipowner Sir Edward Hain in 1911 and restored by Mr J.F. Holman in 1971 as an interdenominational place of worship. St Nicholas is the patron saint of sailors and children. Local Christians hold services at the chapel and welcome visitors. It is a beautiful and peaceful spot. Some of the floor tiles, made by potter Bernard Leach, show fishing scenes.

CARNCROWS STREET

DICK BIDGOOD AND friend in Carncrows Street. The three
parallel streets – Carncrows Street, Teetotal Street
and St Eia Street which branch off from Burrow Road
– were at the heart of St Ives' old fishing quarter of
Downlong. It was a tight-knit community. Most of
the houses had a ground-floor cellar. Since those who
worked for the pilchard seining companies were partly
paid in fish, this cellar was used for salting pilchards,
packing them in barrels called *hogsheads* and pressing
them to produce the valuable *train oil* which had many
uses from tanning leather to fuelling smelly little lamps
called *chills*. Cellars were also used for the storage and
mending of fishing nets. They had a *hepse* door whose top
opened to let in light for net mending while the bottom
stayed shut to keep out marauding cats. The living
quarters began at the top of the outside granite steps.
This area of St Ives was served by little shops which,

in poor fishing seasons, helped out with credit. Other goods were sold from home, as in the fondly recalled notice in a window, *Marinated pilchards for sale. Prepare to meet thy God.* Another read, *Figgie Duff: one penny. More Figgier: a penny halfpenny.*

IN MORE LEISURED times, Carncrows Street basks in the May sunshine. The shutters in Burrow Road give Downlong a Mediterranean atmosphere. The names of Carncrows Street, St Eia Street and Teetotal Street are redolent of St Ives history; Carncrows originates from an ancient cross which stood nearby, St Eia is the patron saint of St Ives. According to the legend, having missed the boat, she sailed across from Ireland on a leaf to convert the Cornish to Christianity. Locals like to assert that she first landed at Hayle, took one look at it and decided to come to St Ives, then called Pendinas, instead. The Teetotal movement supported total abstinence from alcohol. St Ives Teetotal Methodist Society was founded in 1842. Its chapel, which still stands in Chapel Street, was later used as a drill hall.

BETHESDA HILL

BETHESDA HILL LINKS the Wharf and Back Roads (St Ives has a Back Road East and a Back Road West, locally known as Back Roads). Its name may derive from a little chapel at the bottom where a Band of Hope Society was started in 1870. St Ives' town crier and poet, the blind Charlie Paynter, sometimes preached here. The Band of Hope movement was started in Leeds in 1847 after the death of a young man from alcohol. At that time of great poverty, many poor people's lives were destroyed by alcohol, which was seen as a real social evil. The Band of Hope became a national organisation in 1855. Its members *signed the pledge* to refrain from alcohol. An alternative origin of Bethesda Hill's name is that, like the Bethesda in the Bible, referred to in John's Gospel, Chapter 5, it had five porches.

HOLIDAYMAKERS WALK HOME up Bethesda Hill. The building on the left with the lifebuoy was formerly the net loft of the Stevens family's fishing boats *Girl Renee SS 78* and *Francis Stevens SS 49*. It was sympathetically converted to an architect's office. It is an excellent example of one of St Ives' traditional buildings being put to new use but retaining its original character. One of the most photographed streets in St Ives, Bethesda has featured in postcards by Frith, Valentine and Tuck, views which often included the washing drying in the breeze and folksy locals having friendly chats.

THE HARBOUR

COAL CART BY the Harbour Office. Until the Second World War, St Ives was a commercial port as well as a fishing harbour. The main cargo was coal, much of it for the gasworks at Porthmeor. These cargoes often came from Lydney in the Forest of Dean and in later years from Blyth in Northumberland. A coasting schooner, perhaps the local *Susan Elizabeth* or *Mary Waters*, has unloaded some of its cargo into this cart which is being weighed on the weighbridge, used to weigh fish until the 1960s. The second horse which helped to pull the cart up the slipway from the harbour was called a *leader*. John's father remembered coal

being delivered to his home at £1 a cartload and his childhood chore of shovelling it from the back lane into the coal shed. The house behind the cart became famous for Hart's Ice Cream, *Often licked but never beaten.*

DINERS AT THE Sloop Inn. Perhaps no one has evoked this old Inn better than fondly remembered local historian Cyril Noall in his *Beloved St Ives:*

The Sloop, a wonderfully picturesque old Inn which has been sketched, painted and photographed hundreds of times. It was formerly the home of the Williams family and dates from the 17th century. —the Sloop has been much frequented by local artists and numerous examples of their work hung round its walls. —if its old walls could speak, what tales they would have to tell of kegs of smuggled brandy — of golden guineas given as election bribes — of knives flashing suddenly in the smokey lamplight as two foreign sailors engage suddenly in a drunken quarrel for the favours of some harbour side moll.

HARBOUR BEACH

BEN PHILLIPS LOADING fish on the Harbour Beach. Ben, his horse Rose and dog Carlo were the most photographed characters in St Ives. When the fishing boats came in, the catch was put over the side into the punt (small boat). The punt was sculled ashore and the fish loaded into Ben's cart which took it to the Lifeboat Slipway, St Ives' fish market, where it was spread out for sale. The lifeboat slip can be seen sloping down into the harbour on the left. Carlo's role was to run along under the cart where holidaymakers were convinced he was going to get run over. Ben was a big personality with a big voice which could be heard all around the harbour, commenting on the previous Saturday's rugby match. The punt in the photo is from skipper Edwin Stevens' trawler *Francis Stevens SS 49*. Edwin is on the right and his brother Harold on the left. In the centre of the skyline is the chimney of the gasworks at Porthmeor. This space is now filled by St Ives Tate Gallery.

WHERE THERE WERE once rows of boats on the Harbour Beach, locals and visitors enjoy the spring sunshine. Plastic punts are upturned on the little slipway, which is almost covered by sand. Just to the left of the red umbrella is the Fishermen's Coop, formed in 1920 under the energetic leadership of William Lawry who had been a volunteer Fishery Officer at St Ives during the First World War. As suggested by its name, the Coop was owned by the fishermen themselves who paid a minimum of £1 per share. In his delightful book *A Word in Your Ear*, Tom Richards wrote:

> I recall it in the 1930s as an Aladdin's cave, crowded with all manner of interesting things on the counter, the shelves, the floor and suspended from the beams. Oilskins, leather seaboots, lanterns, glass floats, ropes, nets, nails and screws all jostled for space, and over all was the distinctive ... smell of a hardware shop mixed with paraffin and linseed oil.

St Ives used to advertise itself for its *golden sands* and perhaps this photo explains why.

THE LIFEBOAT SLIPWAY

FISH SALE ON the Lifeboat Slipway. Until the twentieth century when it diversified into tourism, St Ives depended on its fisheries. Its luggers sailed as far as Ireland and the North Sea in search of the shoals of herring. St Ives luggers were also built for ports in Ireland, the Isle of Man and the west of Scotland. One was built for Yorkshire. The fish sales on the Lifeboat Slipway were important local events. The fish are laid out for sale by auctioneer Mr J.H. Thomas on the left. They were weighed on the scales, right foreground. With a fish box under his arm is skipper Tommy Toman of the gig *Nellie SS 23*. A former skipper recently recalled how time-consuming it was to land and sell his fish: 'Our fish spent half the day lying around in the sun.' Nowadays the emphasis is on quality. As soon as it has been caught and cleaned the fish is put straight into plastic boxes with ice. Cornish fish has a very high reputation with chefs all over Britain. Much of it is exported, often using Brittany Ferries' Roscoff ferry from Plymouth.

THE OLD LIFEBOAT Slipway is now the place to book your boat trip. St Ives pleasure boats sail to Seal Island (the name invented by local boatmen for this large rock known to fishermen as the Western Carracks), around the Bay or on fishing trips. Or you can do it yourself and hire a self-drive boat. Older St Ives residents remember a more leisurely era when the pleasure boats were graceful sailing yachts – the *Mamie*, *Seagull*, *Hyacinth* and *Gladys May*. Several of St Ives' modern pleasure boats are high-speed craft which dash frantically back and forth along the coast. Self-drive boats were once traditional wooden rowing boats. In the 1960s

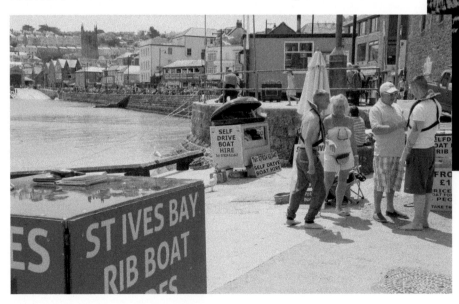

they were fitted with often temperamental outboard motors. Modern self-drive boats are purpose built and whiz about like dodgems. Until the present lifeboat house and slipway were built in 1994, St Ives lifeboat was launched at this slipway after a lengthy trundle along the Wharf Road from the former boathouse at Market Strand, now the Alba restaurant. The Alba gets its name from a famous shipwreck on Porthmeor Beach in 1938 when the St Ives lifeboat *Caroline Parsons* was lost.

PAINTING *EN PLEIN AIR*

WHEN THE ARTISTS began to come to St Ives and Newlyn in the late nineteenth century, painting *en plein air* (outside in the open air, from life) was part of their ethos, in the tradition of the French painter Bastien Lepage. This tradition continued until after the Second World War. Here the artist is working by the One and All lodge, one of five fishermen's lodges including the Rose, Shore Shelter, Shamrock and Bay View. The lodges, founded in the early twentieth century and believed to be unique to St Ives, were meeting places for men only. St Ives wives were known to complain that their men spent more time in the lodge than at home.

Three lodges, the Rose, Shore Shelter and Shamrock, are still used. Their use has diversified. The Shamrock has been used by the Sailing Club. The Rose and Shore Shelter host surgeries by the local MP and the Shore Shelter is also used for evening lessons in the Cornish language. The One and All was washed into the harbour during a storm in 1931. The Bay View at the top of the old wooden pier – the Rampers – was destroyed by a storm. In the foreground of the photo is a boat's mast and a pair of iron wheels, used for launching boats which were often repaired here.

IT IS NOW rare to see artists painting outside unless the School of Painting gives its students an outdoor assignment. As happened during the foundation years of the Art Colony, artists still come here from all over the world, attracted by St Ives' beauty, artistic tradition and special north-facing light. American Arthur Oram from Pewaukee, Wisconsin, has painted here for thirty years. He is one of the few to maintain the tradition of painting outdoors. Arthur can often be seen painting on the Wharf outside the Pool Club. His portraits and landscapes are very popular.

PUNTS

ALL FISHING BOATS had a punt which was used to take its crew aboard and for landing the catch. Sometimes it was a lifeboat. When the St Ives lugger *Mary Ann SS 495* was sunk by German U-boat *UC 65* commanded by Otto Steinbrinck on 8 February 1917, her crew were saved from their punt by the steamer *Sheerness*. There was a huge slaughter of fishing vessels off the North Cornish coast including seven in one day on 30 January 1917 and ten on 12 March. When skipper Matthew Stevens had a new boat built at Porthleven in 1919 she was named *Sheerness* after their rescuer. When the fishing boat *Twin Boys SS 115* was lost on the Three Stone Oar rock near Pendeen Lighthouse on 8 May 1924, her six crew got into their punt and eventually landed safely on the sand

near Zennor. After climbing the cliff, they walked home to St Ives. When the punt was not in use, it was often borrowed by the crew's children. Learning to *scully* with one oar over the stern was an important skill.

ST IVES JUMBO Association is committed to reviving local maritime traditions, including the skill of sculling a punt with one oar over the stern. The Association has held several *Scully Days* to teach this skill. Even some local fishermen no longer know how it's done. For many St Ives boys learning to scully was part of growing up. As the St Ives fishing fleet declined, many of them borrowed punts from the visiting Breton fishermen who came from Camaret and Audierne every year, in their colourful French crabbers, to fish for crawfish and lobsters. Convinced that they were speaking excellent French, the boys would ask *Batoo* (*bateau*) *Johnnie* to borrow the Bretons' punts. Often they borrowed the French punts without permission and the Bretons would stand at the end of Smeaton's Pier yelling for them to bring their punt back!

LUGGERS

LUGGERS AGROUND IN the harbour, drying their sails. Sails had to be carefully looked after and dried to prevent mildew. The *Perseverance SS 40*, known as the *Percy*, had a long fishing career. She was built in 1887 for fisherman William Thomas and C.C. Ross who was a local banker and Member of Parliament during the 1880s. With the rest of the local fishing fleet she was fitted with an engine during the First World War. After the sinking of the *Mary Ann* in 1917, the local motor luggers *Perseverance*, *White Heather*, *Gratitude*, *Helena Maud*, *Mayflower* and *Snowdrop* were fitted with guns to defend themselves against German U-boats. In 1925 the *Perseverance* helped to save the *Provider SS 49* which hit a rock near Land's End. In 1945 the *Perseverance* was sold to the Care family, renamed *Moss Rose* and fished for them for ten years before being sold to Falmouth and replaced by the *Lamorna SS 45*.

TRADITIONAL LUGGERS STILL sail from St Ives, the little white jumbos *Celeste* and *William Paynter* seen here aground on their moorings. The name *jumbo*, an ironic one for St Ives' smallest kind of fishing lugger, was devised in the 1880s when London Zoo's elephant Jumbo hit the headlines. Despite his popularity with the children he gave rides to, Jumbo was a handful for his keepers and was sold to America where he was killed by a train. St Ives' modern jumbos have been built by craftsman Jonny Nance for St Ives Jumbo Association, which aims to revive St Ives' maritime traditions and is always looking for new members to sail its iconic boats. There is a great deal of skill attached to sailing with this traditional Cornish lugger rig. Although the lug foresail is a very efficient sail, the drawback is that it has to be lowered and re-set on the other side of the mast every time the boat tacks towards the wind. This needs practise and good co-ordination. The name *Celeste* comes from the *Babar the Elephant* books. William Paynter was St Ives' most famous boat builder.

FISHERMEN

FISHERMEN IN A gig with their crabpots. Most Cornish lobster fishermen used the traditional *withy pot* made from willow canes. Many Cornish coves like Sennen and Port Isaac had special withy gardens where the fishermen cut their withies every year. Because of the heavy groundswell experienced in the shallower waters of the North Cornish coast, St Ives crabpots were made of strong wire. St Ives wire crabpots would last at least two seasons, in contrast to the withy pot's one, though they may not have fished as well. They were dipped in tar to preserve them. Each crabpot was fitted with two baits, one either side of the mouth, fastened with sharpened sticks called *skivvers*. Salt mackerel, which had a vile smell, was preferred for lobsters while fresh gurnards were used to catch crawfish. Gurnards used to be almost exclusively for crabpot bait but recently the British cook has discovered their excellent flavour. The centre fisherman in the photo wears an oilskin apron called a *barwell*. The iron ring on the mast is the *traveller*, used to hoist the sail.

FISHERMAN SIMON FREEMAN with his crabpots on Smeaton's Pier. Nowadays most crabpots are factory-made of steel or plastic, covered in netting. Simon's are *parlour* pots; there is a separate compartment called the *parlour*. Once a lobster finds its way into the *parlour*, escape is impossible. In 2011 Simon built his own fishing boat, the *Keira SS 61*. Modern fishing boats, even the smallest, are usually very well equipped. Crabpots are hauled by a *vee wheel* which grips the rope and hauls it in. Most boats have radios and echo-sounders which give a profile of the seabed and show fish swimming under the boat. Many have GPS for navigating. Modern crabpots can be worked much faster than in the past. In the 1960s a large Cornish crabbing boat worked about 210 crabpots. A big modern crabber works over 1,000.

ST IVES REGATTA

ST IVES REGATTA, 1930s. The annual August regatta and swimming races were popular events. Here the *Ivor* (left), *Mamie* (in the background) and *Seagull* battle it out. The committee boat *Family SS 61* is on the right. These yachts earned their keep taking trippers around the Bay or mackerel fishing. Paynter's stylish *Mamie* was a regular regatta winner. The local paper the *Western Echo* reported on the 1932 regatta:

> The Regatta. A Perfect Picture. *Very calm weather prevailed until the sailing races were due to start, and it was feared that the Regatta part of the programme would have to be postponed. Suddenly a breeze sprang up from the ESE and arrangements were hurriedly made to get the sailing craft ready. The entrance to the harbour looked a perfect picture*

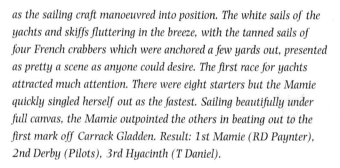

as the sailing craft manoeuvred into position. The white sails of the yachts and skiffs fluttering in the breeze, with the tanned sails of four French crabbers which were anchored a few yards out, presented as pretty a scene as anyone could desire. The first race for yachts attracted much attention. There were eight starters but the Mamie quickly singled herself out as the fastest. Sailing beautifully under full canvas, the Mamie outpointed the others in beating out to the first mark off Carrack Gladden. Result: 1st Mamie (RD Paynter), 2nd Derby (Pilots), 3rd Hyacinth (T Daniel).

IN A STIFF breeze Redwing dinghies race off the harbour. Sailing has come a long way in St Ives since the graceful tripper yachts of the 1930s, though regattas no longer attract hundreds of enthusiastic spectators. When the Redwing class came to visit from Mount's Bay after the war, they easily defeated all of St Ives' traditional yachts. At present, St Ives has a small but friendly sailing club which sails in St Ives Bay as often as the weather allows. In the spring and summer, sailing is on Wednesday evenings and Saturday afternoons. The club has its own safety boat and a little cabin at its boatyard in the Sloop car park where members' boats are kept. Visiting sailors are welcome. Sometimes the boats are accompanied by the dolphins which visit St Ives Bay. The club is generously supported by sponsorship from local organisations.

BACK ROAD EAST

MATT PEARCE SELLING vegetables from his pony and trap in Back Road East, facing Sea View Place. A popular local character, Matt is affectionately remembered crying his wares around Downlong. Matt's portrait was sketched and painted several times by local artist Hyman Segal, most famously in his large painting 'Dominoes at the Sloop' which included several other well-known local characters, among them Gascoigne Paynter, Tommy Andrews and Willie *Sailor* Stevens. Matt's pony and trap would have a hard time in St Ives' contemporary August traffic jams. Another St Ives hawker sold fish with his cry of, 'Fresh hake and whiting!' Fish hawkers were known as *jousters*, a Cornish dialect word.

BACK ROAD EAST and Sea View Place. St Ives
abounds with quaint streets. In most of these
former fishing families' cottages, the cellars
have been converted into kitchens. Fortunately
the attractive iron railings and granite steps
have been retained. From the 1960s, local
families moved out of these small cottages to
more modern and spacious houses in the upper
part of the town. But holidaymakers love the
atmosphere of these little dwellings, which have
been refurbished to meet their needs. Many
of them have been given folksy and nautical
names to attract the self-catering customer,
so a tour of Downlong is likely to reveal
Pilchard Cottage, Breton Cottage, Cobblestones,
Midships, Wheelhouse, Seal Cottage, Ship's Cat,
Anchorage, Mariners and Shell Cottage.
Avast me hearties! There is even a Salmon's
Leap though St Ives was not famous for its
salmon fishery. The one problem visitors might
experience is where to park, as Downlong was
built long before the motor car appeared. Huge
sums of money have been paid for parking
spaces in St Ives. Recently a single space near
the centre of town was sold for £56,000.

DOWNLONG

OFF TO SCHOOL in the 1940s. Downlong had its own infant school near the Island. In 1881 the Board School was built on the edge of town and parents complained about how far their children had to walk. Washing was hung in the street using a clothes prop. There were no gardens Downlong for hanging out washing. In those days, wash day was a serious business. The washing was often put in the washtray to soak on Sunday night. A bar of soap was flaked into washing flakes with a knife. First thing on Monday morning, a fire was lit under the copper, out in the scullery. Whites were boiled clean. Stubborn stains were scrubbed on the washboard in the washtray. Next the sopping washing was put through the wooden rollers of the iron mangle with its business-like cogs to squash out much of the water and a good many buttons. Next the clothes were put in the oval wash basket, the *flasket*, and hung out to dry. When not in use the rectangular washtray was often borrowed by the boys and paddled around the harbour as a boat. There was even a washtray race in the local regatta!

FEW FAMILIES NOW live Downlong where most of the cottages have been converted to self-catering holiday lets. But Downlong remains unspoiled. Our modern photographer, Barrie, has successfully captured the atmosphere of the previous archive photograph which was probably taken by Mousehole photographer Geraldine Underell, who loved to capture the sunshine and shadows of our narrow Cornish streets. Where the scooter was once parked there is now a wheelie bin. While the wheelie bin may not fit the aesthetics of this area, it has been a great success in dealing with the problem of rampaging seagulls which have no problem getting into plastic bin bags. But the gull problem is manmade. Café owners discovered that they could earn a few extra pennies selling their stale bread to feed the gulls. The fast-food outlets provide a ready lunch for enterprising gulls. Unfortunately many people have been attacked by gulls who steal their ice creams or chips. Visitors are now warned: Do not feed the gulls. Cover your food.

Now the seagull's joined the gentry,
Its diet is refined.
No longer its contented
With what the fishers leave behind
It seeks out the best shop pasties
For fudge it is a killer
And when it comes to ice cream
It has to be Vanilla!

NETTING

FROM THE SECOND World War, making camouflage nets was an important domestic industry. They were made using a wooden net needle and a board called a *measter* to give the size of the mesh. This can be seen on the right in the image below. The nets were taken to the Island Factory for strips of coloured cloth to be inserted. Susie Freeman, left, and Meryl Noall, right, are at work outside the Freeman's house in Victoria Place. On the left are Margaret Freeman and Amy Perkin. Making and mending nets was an important skill. One local remembered that when he came home from school, he had to make enough crab net to fill up the window, before he went out to play. Crab nets had big meshes so making them was not as time-consuming as other kinds of nets. It is easy to make a net,

but mending one is much harder. The skill is to cut out a space which could be meshed in in one go. Every fishermen carried a knife used for *cutting out* in net mending.

CHRIS *BISH* CARE runs his net setting business from the historic Porthmeor Studios, recently restored to provide studios for the artists and net lofts for the fishermen. Chris was much involved in this restoration as a doughty and eloquent representative of the fishermen. Here Chris explains to a group of schoolchildren how a net is set, i.e. fastened, to its ropes. These gill nets are used to catch white fish like pollack, hake and turbot. The market for pollack and hake has expanded with better information, promoted by celebrity chefs, about other kinds of fish than the well-known cod. Chris fished from Newlyn in the St Ives netter *Keriolet SS 114* with skipper Andrew *Traz* Treloar. His father and uncles worked the Care family's boats *Moss Rose SS 40* and *Lamorna SS 45*. These boats fished with baited lines which stretched for miles along the seabed and were called *long lines*. Netting has entirely replaced long lining.

SERVICES
ON THE
SLIPWAY

THE SALVATION ARMY'S Sunday
evening services on the Lifeboat Slipway
were well attended by large crowds of
visitors who enthusiastically joined
in singing lively popular hymns like
'Blessed Assurance Jesus is Mine',
'Will Your Anchor hold in the Storms
of Life?' and 'Eternal Father Strong
to Save'. The evening began with
the Army's stirring march along the
Wharf Road, behind its band and flag,
from its Citadel to the Slipway. It had
many excellent musicians and lively
preachers. Its services on the Slipway
were very popular, with the crowd
overflowing onto the road, but the crowd
in this photo was even bigger than usual.

THE SLIPWAY AREA is still used for Christian witness. Here the young people of the United Beach Mission, regular visitors to St Ives, dressed in their familiar red shirts, speak to those gathered. The Beach Mission also holds regular events on Porthminster Beach. It is supported by members of local churches. The organisation is based in Leeds and has been at work for sixty years. Every year it organises ninety missions in the British Isles and Europe.

CHOIRS

PRIMITIVE METHODIST CHOIR outing, 1905. Choir
members pose for the camera, all dressed in their Sunday best.
Fore Street Primitive Methodist Church and St Peter's Street
Bible Christian Church were at the centre of many St Ives
people's lives. They still play a very lively role in the life of
the community. Their Sunday schools are active and well
supported. These churches were famous for their music,
fervent hymns sung in four-part harmony. The Bible
Christian movement was founded by William O'Bryan.
Its St Peter's Street Church was built in 1824 and enlarged
in 1858. Fore Street Church was built by the harbour in 1831.
Blue elvan (the local name for greenstone) rocks, used in the
construction, were brought by fishing boat from Porthmeor
Cove, near Gurnard's Head, and carried to the site by women
in their aprons. Another tradition is that the wooden pillars,
which support the gallery, were spare masts given by the
skippers of the fishing luggers.

ON A WARM June evening St Ives Community Choir stages an impromptu rehearsal on the steps of the Island chapel. Harmonious strains of 'What a Wonderful World' drift across St Ives Bay, welcoming locals and visitors alike to this spot. Musical Director William Thomas guides the singers with popular tunes, both religious and secular. William is a strong advocate of singing. He says, 'it improves health, encourages social inclusion and breaks down barriers.' Choir members are: kneeling, William Thomas. *First row, from left to right:* Joan Rowe, Alan Thomas, Barbara Warner. *Second row:* Alison Ashby, Mary Paynter, John Lander, Jane Perkin, Norma Churchward. *Third row:* Heather Greaves, Judith Tremelling, Joan Symons, Steve Bassett, Chloe Harding, Marguerite Butcher, Lesley Thomas. *Fourth row:* Angela Charleston, Lynda Thomas, Derek Churchward, Jenny Duda, Rachel Knowles, Patricia Thomas, Lynda Morlaine. *Fifth row:* Margaret Trevorrow, Margaret Cartwright, Sophie Wilkinson, Maureen Stevens, Don Stevens, Mike Laramy, Lynne Brereton, Johanna Evans, Sue Doggeth, Vicky Taylor, Rita Coop, Wendy Berriman.

BUNKERS HILL

BUNKERS HILL TAKES its name from the battle in the American War of Independence on 17 June 1775. Previously it was called Bolton Street after the Duke of Bolton who owned property in St Ives. The Bolton property in St Ives was sold in June 1904, four cottages in Bunkers Hill and Bailey's Lane going for £300. In those pre-refrigeration days, fish (rays) dry in the sun while a fish jouster's (hawker's) horse takes a well-deserved lunch. This photo was taken from the site of St Ives' best-known bakery, Ferrell's. Further up the hill, on the corner of Rose Lane, was Mr Tanner the basket-maker, who wove *maunds* for the fishing industry.

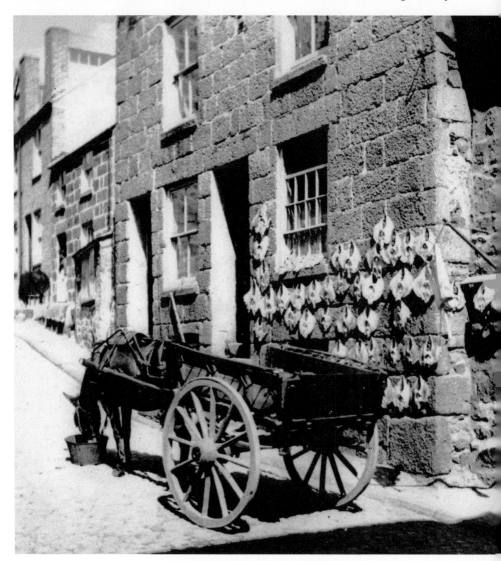

Bunkers Hill was once the location of one of St Ives' many pilchard seine cellars: Brooking Williams. All St Ives' pilchard seine boats were tarred black and almost identical. To tell them apart, special marks of stripes, bars, circles or diamond shapes were painted on the bows. Brooking Williams seine company's bow mark was a white ball inside a white ring. It looked a bit like a target or dart board. These distinctive bow marks often appeared in contemporary paintings of the seiners fishing in the Bay.

BUNKERS HILL FROM the top end. At the bottom is Fore Street Methodist Church. Like many of St Ives' cobbled streets, Bunkers Hill often has colourful floral displays. On the right is Fore Street Church Sunday school room. Work started on collecting the money for this building in 1904. The foundation stone and memorial stones were laid in the presence of the mayor, Alderman W. Pearce and the superintendent minister the Revd R. Rutter and other guests in 1922. The memorial stones commemorate many stalwarts who supported the church. The building, designed by Mr Wills, was opened a year later. Among those present were the mayor and mayoress (Mr and Mrs Beckerleg), the Revd and Mrs Rutter, Mr James Ninnis, 'Father' Freeman, Mr R. Tanner, Miss K. French, magistrates, aldermen and councillors, Free Church ministers, members of the business and fishing communities and a large crowd of members who filled the little street.

CARVINGS

UNCLE MANUEL CARVING a model boat in Love Lane. Uncle Manuel was a highly skilled craftsman and the model lugger which he has completed, on the left, is a faithful representation of a mackerel boat, the bigger class of St Ives fishing boat, beautifully carved and painted and accurately rigged. The model under construction is fitted with a keel which shows that she is intended to sail and not just for decoration. St Ives was a maritime town and model boats and model boat racing were taken very seriously. The ancient tradition of sailing model boats on Consols Pool, at the top of the Stennack, every Good Friday, is still strongly supported. And Consols Pool Association is determined to keep the tradition alive. A few years ago when the Pool was choked with weed on Good Friday, the local community was furious and quick to tell the local council what they thought about it.

CRAFTSMAN STEVE MARTIN carves contemporary versions of St Ives' traditional wooden dolls called Joannies. They represent local personalities, including the mayor, a rugby player, a fisherman and policewoman. Some of Steve's friends have been lucky enough to receive Joannies of themselves. Originally, Joannies were crafted from the ends of broken oars. The head was carved from the narrow handle part of the oar and the body from the wider part. However, not enough oars are broken in St Ives to supply Steve nowadays! Steve has been very successful in reviving and popularising this old folk toy. A recent housing development in the upper town was named Joannies Avenue. The Victorian practitioner of this craft was William Barber who lived in Pudding Bag Lane, now the Sloop car park. Pudding Bag Lane got its name from its shape; like a pudding bag there was only one way in. William had only one eye. When he retired from fishing, he kept busy making Joannies for the children who lived in Downlong. St Ives Museum, which is well worth a visit, has an excellent collection of old Joannies. These have darker and more restrained colours than Steve's cheerful modern versions, but lots of character. Perhaps other contemporary craftsmen will produce their own take on this old Cornish toy?

THE OLD ARCH

THE OLD ARCH near the Digey leads into Hicks' Court where formerly stood the residence of the Hicks family. In his excellent and authoritative book *St Ives in Old Picture Postcards*, author William Thomas writes:

> *The house was already in ruins when, in 1892, Matthews wrote in his History of St Ives, —it had evidently been in past times an imposing structure, as was seen by the mullioned bay windows with square hood moulding, at the corners of which were the letters GH for George Hicks.—Immediately to the left of this window was the entrance to a narrow passage through the house, at the other end of which, on the right, was a decrepit oak-panelled door which led to the principal apartments—. Round the walls of the upper storey could still be seen remains of the old panelling, window seats and cupboards, also the fireplaces. The dining room had a vaulted ceiling. Underneath the house was a secret smuggling cave or cellar.*

SITUATED OFF THE Digey, scantle slates adorn the adjoining buildings of this popular much-photographed feature, the Old Arch. Once the gateway to George Hicks' Tudor mansion, the arch is made from three roughly hewn granite slabs. George Hicks was a seventeenth-century businessman and churchwarden. He wrote a history of St Ives, unfortunately since lost. George Hicks featured in the old seventeenth-century Borough Accounts. In 1647 St Ives was hit by the plague, which killed 535 of its people, about a third of the population. The survivors would have starved, since neighbouring farmers would not bring their produce to town and risk catching the plague, but fortunately a ship from Plymouth arrived with a cargo of wheat. The cargo was bought and given away. George Hicks was one of those involved in this transaction. Hicks Court leads off the Digey, whose name continues to puzzle researchers. A possible explanation is Dye Chy, Dye House.

VIRGIN STREET

THIS NINETEENTH-CENTURY scene shows Virgin Street before the top end was built. Many of St Ives' picturesque old streets have puzzling names: Teetotal Street, Mount Zion, Love Lane, and the Digey. Locals much enjoy hearing visitors mispronounce Digey as Diggy. Some earlier street names were even odder, like Dick's Hill (still used by locals to refer to Fish Street) and Street Petite. Those with Cornish names have been translated – Street an Pol: Street with a Pool, Street an Garrow: Rough Street and Stennack: Tin Place. The recently named Parc

an Stamps might be puzzling until you realise that Parc is Cornish for field and stamps were tin-crushing machines. It was thought that Virgin Street might have a religious origin but it is agreed that virgin is in the sense of new. Virgin Street was much changed in 1937 when eleven ancient cottages on the right were replaced by five new ones, carefully built in the vernacular style to fit in with the historic locality. Wouldn't it be great if some more recent building in St Ives was that thoughtful?

VIRGIN STREET, THOROUGHLY smartened up now, with the addition of some social housing. Gone is the towering chimney. A local workman poses to recreate some movement in this formerly busy street.

COURT COCKING

COURT COCKING LOOKING from Fore Street through to the Wharf. In 1970 this area narrowly missed the fire which destroyed four cottages, four cafés, a large shop and a garage. Luckily there were no casualties, except the bull mastiff 'Tory', which had given the first warning of the outbreak. The name Court Cocking is one of a

number of streets, courts and alleyways bearing strange and mysterious names. Here this well-posed image – as was the way in the early twentieth century – shows a young girl with a pinny to keep her 'good' clothes clean and a well-dressed young man. Will he start work with the wheelbarrow, we ask? Other characters, looking rather dour, debate whether it is safe to put out the washing.

NOT MUCH HAS changed in Court Cocking. The windows, though re-glazed, are in the same position and a balcony has been added to the cottage on the left-hand side. Plaques on the left-hand side of the door show which letting agency to contact in order to rent this holiday property. If you do, the views over St Ives harbour will be stunning. This quiet image belies the busy Wharf Road which you will encounter through the arch. Mention the surname Cocking in the streets of St Ives and almost anyone you meet will associate the name with the lifeboat, as several members of this family have been well-known coxswains.

LIFEBOATS

THE ROYAL NATIONAL Lifeboat Institution established
a station in St Ives in 1860 and gifted the first lifeboat
Moses to St Ives the following year. The lifeboat depicted
was a rowing and sailing one and bore the name *Exeter*,
in acknowledgement of the legacy of William Kendal of Exeter.
This boat is the second of the series, stationed at St Ives from
1886 to 1899. Built by Woolfe, of Shadwell, she rowed ten
oars and carried a crew of thirteen. Those appearing in the
photo, taken between 1895–98, are, in the boat, *from left
to right:* Thomas Henry Quick (coxswain), Richard Williams
Stevens, Steve Phillips, Henry David Daniel, Thomas Red Care,
unknown, Tom Hart. Standing by the carriage: Charlie French
(honorary secretary – he appears to be holding a maroon gun),
William Peters, Thomas Daniel, ? Cocking, Chipps Bassett,
Anthony Hart and Peter Lugg. Other celebrated coxswains
and lifeboat men were Paul Curnow and James Murphy, who
between them carried out many gallant services.

ST IVES LIFEBOAT *Princess Royal* (Civil Service No. 41)
in the harbour, on her carriage, with her towing tractor.
The *Princess Royal* entered service at St Ives in 1990.
In May 2013 St Ives lifeboat station received a visit from the

Queen and the Duke of Edinburgh. The *Princess Royal* will be replaced by a new Shannon Class all-weather lifeboat, powered not by propellers but by twin water jets, with a speed of 25 knots and costing £1.5 million. This has been funded by a generous legacy. The Royal National Lifeboat Institution is now appealing for funds to help meet the £1 million cost of the specially designed launch and recovery vehicle that will be needed to go with it. A dedicated band of volunteers open the lifeboat shop next to the boathouse to sell souvenirs and raise much-needed funds for the cause. With the wonderful summer weather of 2013 and the massive use of our splendid beaches, for swimming and boating, the lifeboat and its inshore partner have been in much demand.

FORE STREET

JUBILEE CELEBRATIONS OF King George V in Fore Street in 1935. Fore Street is still one of St Ives' busiest thoroughfares. During this time, the street contained, among other businesses, a printers, a taxidermist, a butcher, a surgery, an ironmonger and the Star Tea Company. The surgery on the extreme left was that of Dr J.M. Nicholls JP, who died in 1937. He was Mayor of St Ives in 1892 and Medical Officer of Health for over

forty years. This busy gentleman was a Cornwall County Councillor and a much-loved figure in the town. Further down the street on the right, a printing business and stationery shop was run by James Uren White. He had moved to St Ives in 1892 and published the first local newspaper the *St Ives Weekly Summary*. The chemist, Leddras, is still there. This lovely watercolour was painted by St Ives artist Winifred Freeman and can be viewed at St Ives Guildhall.

FORE STREET, NOW a one-way street, and one of the main shopping streets in the town, is crowded at most times of the year. Unsuspecting pedestrians scuttle to the sides, when traffic, mostly delivery vans, struggles through. The genre of shops has distinctly changed to clothing, surf items, art galleries, gift shops, pasties, cafés, pubs and restaurants. In the season crowds flock to this area and it is not unknown to be buffeted by a stray backpack.

MARKET PLACE

IN 1797, JOHN Knill, a former mayor and customs officer, drew up a trust deed instituting a quinquennial ceremony on St James' Day – 25 July, in which ten little girls would dance around his intended mausoleum on Worvas Hill. The parade, here passing through Market Place, would be accompanied by a fiddler, two elderly widows and three trustees – the mayor, customs officer and vicar of St Ives. These worthy locals were Captain T. Row Harry (mayor), the Revd S.F. Marsh (vicar), Mr H. Fook (collector of customs, Falmouth), Mr T. Curnow (fiddler), Frances Honor Butler, Frances Phillips, Mary J. Watty, Elizabeth Thomas Tanner, Grace Burt, Susan Watty Humphries, Emily Andrews, Bessie Veal, Phillipa Chard and Clara Peters (little girls), Elizabeth Honey and Margaret Jeffery (widows) and Mr P.J.W. Hawke (MC). The first ceremony took place in 1801 and this image is dated 1901. Continuing today, the next Knill's ceremony will be in 2016.

TOURIST SHOPS AND a Chinese restaurant replace the chemist and teashop. The ubiquitous yellow lines are visible on the street. They adorn much of the town. This unusually quiet aspect of the street will be choc-a-bloc when the season takes hold. One is reminded of the history of this area – Market Place. Just out of shot stands

the Market House and is known as the hub of St Ives town. The first Market House, then
known as St Ives Guildhall, was made of wood and built in 1490 by Sir Robert Willoughby,
an influential land owner, in the same century as St Ives Parish Church. It has had a
chequered life as the market as there were few shops in the town at that time. Later it
contained the magistrates' court, where the town mayor would serve as chief magistrate of
the day, and the town gaol which could accommodate ten prisoners. Their crimes would be
mainly thievery and drunkenness. The unfortunate John Payne who had served as the town
mayor and magistrate was hanged in Market Place in 1549 because he joined the Cornish
Rebel Army to fight against the introduction of the new English prayer book. In 1832 the
building was rebuilt as the fine granite edifice we know today and was again put in good
repair in 1978. Now upstairs is a social club and downstairs is divided into a number of
small shops.

BARNOON HILL

BARNOON HILL, C.1890. This view is down the hill towards the tower of the Parish Church of St Ia. The first building on the left was a Navigation School run by Captain J.T. Short, the diarist, who as a young man spent ten years of captivity in Napoleon's France. The Navigation School was demolished in 1910 to make way for an early cinema – the Picturedrome, which later became the Palais de Danse. The steps immediately below led to Mr William Bryant's carpenter's shop, whilst further down was the shoemaker's shop of Mr Farrell. The Palais de Danse was eventually acquired by Miss Barbara Hepworth, the world-famous sculptor, as her studio. She lived in a house nearly opposite, by the entrance to Ayr Lane.

THIS WELL-TRODDEN hill near the centre of town, Barnoon Hill, shows steps to the left to ease the gradient for the less agile. Bottom right is the house by the entrance to Ayr Lane where Barbara Hepworth lived. After her death in 1973 the house was converted to the Barbara Hepworth Museum and Sculpture Garden. The Sculpture Garden behind the house once formed part of the grounds of Trewyn, residence of the Trewhella family. The Barbara Hepworth Museum is affiliated to Tate St Ives. Across the road, the former Palais de Danse, which once was said to have the 'best sprung dance floor in Cornwall', is now used as storage for the Tate. On the hill behind the Parish Church tower is a new white building, yet to be occupied. It is next to the Malakoff Bus Station.

BARBARA HEPWORTH

DAME BARBARA HEPWORTH (1903–1975) carving her stone sculpture 'Vertical Form' in the yard at Trewyn Studio. Barbara Hepworth bought the studio with its secluded walled garden in 1949 and there she lived and worked for the rest of her life. In 1968, she and the potter Bernard Leach received the Freedom of St Ives. The citation described the sculptor as being a truly eminent artist living and working in the community. After her tragic death in a fire during 1973 her house and garden became a museum devoted to her work.

ST IVES HAS the good fortune to display several of Barbara Hepworth's sculptures around the town. This is 'Epidaurous' at the Malakoff, overlooking the sea. Dame Barbara donated this sculpture to St Ives in 1961. Barbara Hepworth was awarded the CBE in the New Year's Honours List of 1958 and was made a Dame in 1965. She received many more honours from universities. She was a trustee of the Tate Gallery from 1965–1972. During celebrations of Dame Barbara's 70th birthday, Epidaurous, a bronze sculpture, made its appearance at the Malakoff where the Round Table had created a garden. The sculpture was offered on permanent loan, after the designer of the scheme, Henry Gilbert, had interested Barbara Hepworth in the project. 'Come round and choose whatever you like,' she said.

THE SCALA CINEMA

BUILT ON THE site of the Queens Hotel stables, the Scala Cinema was opened in 1920. This of course was in the days of silent movies. These movies were accompanied by a pianist or sometimes a small orchestra. From 8*d* to 2*s* 4*d* was charged to enjoy the marvels in the cinema which was described as 'The chief centre of amusement in St Ives'. The cinema was decorated with magnificent galleons and other sea-faring themes. They were expertly painted by John Rankine Barclay. Born in Edinburgh, he began work as an engraver, then became a student at the Royal Scottish Academy Schools in 1908, winning the Guthrie award and a Carnegie Travelling Scholarship. Barclay moved to Cornwall in 1935, living at Zennor, and was known for his decorative and mural paintings. French Impressionism

was a great influence on him. He was a versatile artist, also producing woodcuts and book illustrations. His work included landscapes of London parks, Cornish harbours and moor scenes. John Barclay joined the St Ives Society of Artists after the Second World War and was elected to its council, becoming secretary in 1958 and retiring shortly before his death in 1964. He assisted Leonard Fuller at the St Ives School of Painting and proved to be a kind critic and encouraging to newcomers.

SHOPPERS HURRY PAST the old Scala Cinema in High Street, now Boots the Chemist. Fortunately the front has retained its 1920 design. High Street separates Tregenna Place and Market Place and is one of the main thoroughfares in the town. The Lanham's business in High Street is still flourishing. Established in 1869 as a wine merchants and supplier of artists' materials, its proprietor provided the St Ives artists with their first picture gallery. Lanham's now is a self-catering holiday and property management company.

THE GUILDHALL

IN 1927 MRS Elizabeth Noy bequeathed 5,000 guineas for the erection of a new municipal building. This resulted in the opening in 1940 of the Guildhall in Street an Pol. This attractive edifice with a balcony overlooking a spacious forecourt has served the town well, the concert hall being a particularly valuable amenity. The concert shown is being given by The Mission Minstrels, accompanied by John T. Barber, well-known St Ives poet and musician. The Seaman's Mission, now the Museum, was the social focus of Downlong at the time. The Smeaton's pier back-cloth on the stage was painted by Marsden Prophet, and oversaw many pleasurable entertainments.

A CHRISTMAS FAIR at St Ives Guildhall. Shoppers are entertained by the rock choir on stage. Every Thursday there is a farmers' market selling quality local produce ranging from home-made bread to St Ives beer, Cornish-caught fish, honey and, of course, the essential pasties. The Guildhall hosts concerts and many other events including the National Judo Easter weekend, beer festivals, wedding receptions, discos and country dancing. During the town's popular annual St Ives September Festival, the Festival Committee produces a huge programme of musical events to cater for all tastes. There are also open studios and free pub entertainment. The venues include St Ives Arts Club, the Parish Church, the Western Hotel, St Ives Library as well as the Guildhall. Talks, workshops, tours, films, exhibitions, plays and theatre and poetry are all available during the Festival Fortnight. The Guildhall also accommodates the Visitors' Information Centre and St Ives Council Meeting Rooms and Council Offices.

TREGENNA HILL

NOTHING CHANGES. BUSES jostle for space at the top of Tregenna Hill, where it meets Fern Lea Terrace. Eileen's Café on the left was a very popular meeting place. On the right, the Roman Catholic church of the Sacred Heart and St Ia, built in 1908, to a design by A.J.C. Scholes, overlooks the mayhem. Tregenna Hill was built in the early 1800s as a good-class residential thoroughfare, but gradually the houses were converted into shops, making it today one of the busiest shopping streets in the town.

A TRIP TO Land's End from St Ives on an open-top bus is a summer treat. The journey takes an hour and a half, and meanders through the West Cornwall countryside. Bus drivers are well-versed on how to deal with St Ives' narrow streets. The redundant telephone box has made a comeback as an advertising booth.

ST IVES PARISH CHURCH

ST IVES PARISH Church, *c*.1900. This fifteenth-century church was dedicated to St Ia and St Andrew. It was built with granite brought by sea from Zennor. St Ia was an Irish princess who introduced Christianity to this district in the fifth century. She had missed her fellow missionaries leaving from Ireland to Cornwall and, saddened, she knelt down and prayed. As she did so she noticed a little leaf which expanded and would take her weight on the water. Trustingly she embarked on the leaf and was wafted across the Channel, reaching her destination before the others. The people among whom she settled were fishermen who accepted her Christian teaching. In return they also adopted her name. The place became known as Porthia – Ia's Cove, which was anglicised to St Ie's. It is not known where the intrusive 'v' came from. There is certainly no connection between the Cornish St Ives and the one in Huntingdonshire. Beside the church there is a late fifteenth-century cross, re-erected in 1850, having been found buried in the churchyard. The church tower, a prominent

feature in the town, contains two bells which were cast in Hayle Foundry in 1830. Windows in the church were damaged in 1904 by an explosion at Hayle Dynamite Works. On the left is the Star Inn in St Andrews Street. Legend suggests that members of the church orchestra repaired here for liquid refreshment during the sermon.

A STREETLIGHT HELPS frame the image at the entrance to St Andrews Street, next to St Ia Church. The road is widened and on the left are the memorial gardens, built on land donated by Sir Edward Hain. Sir Edward Hain, founder of the Hain Steamship Co., was a great benefactor to the town and was its mayor on several occasions. Lady Hain, too, was noted for her good works. An endowment of £8,000 allowed a hospital to be opened in 1920. This was the

Edward Hain Memorial Hospital in memory of Sir Edward Hain's son, Captain Edward Hain, who was killed at Gallipoli in the First World War. Signs advertise the weekly market in the Parish Rooms. Reader – please forgive us for a commercial moment. If you have reached here, you've missed a wonderful opportunity to visit St Ives Archive, nearby.

ST IVES RAILWAY STATION

ST IVES RAILWAY Station. The development of the
tourist industry was made possible by the opening of
the branch railway from St Erth in 1877. A vigorous
advertising campaign, which proved very successful,
was conducted by the Great Western Railway. For
instance, 'The Swindon Week', when the GWR closed its
locomotive and carriage works for the holidays, was an
eagerly anticipated event. In July 1934, 1,200 passengers
came to St Ives from Swindon. This train has brought
a large number of passengers to enjoy the sunshine on
Porthminster Beach. The area behind the beach huts
would have held the seine boats, relics of a once great local
fishing industry.

THE ST IVES Branch Line survived the notorious Beeching Axe of 1963 which closed so many rural railways. A special treat for railway buffs is the arrival of a classic steam locomotive. In this photograph by St Ives Archive volunteer, the late Keith Lloyd, the locomotive *Lancashire Fusilier* heads the St Ives steamer from Penzance to St Ives on 24 March 2007. A happy moment occurred in June 2013, when Her Majesty, Queen Elizabeth II and the Duke of Edinburgh visited St Ives for the first time. They travelled, with the regular patrons, on the branch line from St Erth to St Ives, which is considered to be one of the prettiest in the UK.

PORTHMINSTER

THE HAMLET OF Porthminster survived burning by the French in the time of Henry VI.
For centuries this cove was the centre of pilchard seine fishing. Pilchard seining took place
in the autumn, when vast shoals entered the sandy coves adjacent to the town and were
trapped inside the huge seine nets shot around them. During Victorian times, however,
the beach began to be used by an increasing number of bathers. During the 1880s ladies'
bathing tents had been installed on the beach, whilst the men and boys had staked out

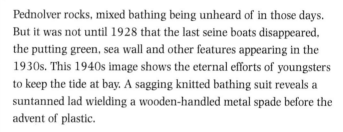

Pednolver rocks, mixed bathing being unheard of in those days. But it was not until 1928 that the last seine boats disappeared, the putting green, sea wall and other features appearing in the 1930s. This 1940s image shows the eternal efforts of youngsters to keep the tide at bay. A sagging knitted bathing suit reveals a suntanned lad wielding a wooden-handled metal spade before the advent of plastic.

THIS CRESCENT OF golden sand, framed by a glittering bay, has glorious views across to Godrevy Lighthouse, inspiration for Virginia Woolf's novel *To the Lighthouse*. With the benefit of the mildest climate in the UK along with waving palm trees and translucent waters, there is a definite tropical feel to the place. Located just a short walk from the centre of St Ives, the award-winning Blue Flag beach at Porthminster is a family favourite for safe swimming while onshore you can simply relax in a deck chair or try your skill at the mini eighteen-hole golf course where you can also order up freshly made juices and smoothies. There is a car park overlooking the beach, but this can get very busy. Try parking at St Erth or Lelant Saltings and enjoy the scenic branch line that runs right into St Ives and a short stroll down to the beach. A seasonal dog ban applies on this beach. Here a family – all wearing hats and, no doubt, smothered in factor 30 – enjoys Porthminster Beach. Dad adjusts the architecture of the serious business of castle building and Mum takes the photos. Happy days!

PORTHMINSTER BEACH

THE NAME PORTHMINSTER suggests the presence of a monastery at this cove. John Hobson Matthews states there was a chapel here at the point where the stream crosses the beach; its foundations were exposed around 1870 during a flood, together with two stone coffins and leaden chalices, which were deposited in a local museum. Matthews states, 'I have never seen them'. Neither, apparently, has anyone else. In Victorian times the regatta was the high spot of the summer. This popular event of swimming and sailing competitions, on Porthminster Beach, was keenly contested to gain awards and prizes. The rocks below Pednolva Hotel are crowded to allow for a better view. The Salvation Army Band entertains those less interested in the water activities.

PORTHMINSTER BEACH WAS a frenzy of activity on 29 June 2013 with the Love Architecture St Ives event, part of a series of events throughout the UK. This Big Build sandcastle competition was sponsored by a local architectural firm. A truly community event saw families, friends and businesses working together. The beach café, as well as selling ice cream and other sea-side delights, hosts barbeques on summer nights. At the far end of the beach is award-winning restaurant Porthminster Beach Café.

HURLING OF
THE SILVER BALL

THE HURLING OF the silver ball, 1930. This event takes place on the first Monday after 3 February, and is one of the few games of hurling now played only by children. This early snap shows a short-lived attempt to provide a goal and rules for the proceedings. This quaint custom celebrates Feast Sunday, the anniversary of the dedication of the Parish Church. Lelant Feast falls on 2 February. This made it possible for St Ives to play Lelant at hurling on their common holiday of Feast Monday. The silver hurling ball used to be thrown to the players near a stone marking the St Ives and Lelant parish boundary, the two goals being their respective churches. As the population of St Ives increased, Lelant began to find itself outnumbered in the game, and dropped out. Hurling was thereafter confined to the young men of St Ives. Picking teams was easy. Those with the Christian names of Thomas, William or John were on one team and those with any other Christian name on the other. In this way the game continued to be played for many years.

IN 1972 THE event was reorganised, reviving its old spirit and character. Early on Feast Monday the silver ball is carried in state to the holy well of St Ia at Porthmeor, where it is immersed and blessed. The ball is borne on a cushion of ivy through the old part of town in a procession which includes the vicar, the mayor and macebearers. Following a reception at the Guildhall, the mayor then leads the procession to the churchyard where he stands by the wall and throws the ball to the waiting players below with the cry in Cornish, of 'Guare wheg ya guare teg', 'fair play is good play'. Here, in 2012, the mayor Ron Tulley, assisted by macebearer Alan Major, hurls the ball over the church wall onto the beach below. The winner usually passes the ball to a younger relative, to be returned to the mayor at noon at the Guildhall when a gift is given. New pennies are also thrown for all the assembled children. This Feast Day celebrates the consecration of the Parish Church in 1434.

CELEBRATIONS

THE VERY IDEA of a day that would *'remind children that they formed part of the British Empire, and that they might think with others in lands across the sea, what it meant to be sons and daughters of such a glorious Empire'*, and that *'The strength of the Empire depended upon them, and they must never forget it'*, had been considered as early as 1897. The image of a motherly Queen Victoria, Empress of India, as its paramount ruler, would be shared by an Empire spanning almost a quarter of the entire globe. However, it was not until after the death of Queen Victoria, who died on 22 January 1901, that Empire Day was first celebrated. The first 'Empire Day' took place on 24 May 1902, the queen's birthday. Although not officially recognised as an annual event until 1916, many schools across the British Empire were celebrating it before then. One New Zealand school journal

from 1910 records: *This is the 'Union Jack'; and now that Empire Day has come round once more, you will hear its history. It is really a coloured picture from a history-book, telling of things that happened, long before you were born.* This 1940s image shows a group of St Ives children outside the Board School in the Stennack celebrating the day. Millions of children from all walks of life across the British Empire would salute the flag and sing patriotic songs. For them the highlight of the day was that they were let out of school early. Taking part on this occasion were Mary Veal, Phyllis Philips, Valerie Stevens by the flag, Joyce Harvey, Sarah Bennetts with drum, Graham Curnow, Arthur Eddy, Matthew Whitford and Donald Stevens.

IN 1977 THE Queen's silver jubilee was marked with celebrations at every level throughout the country and Commonwealth. The actual anniversary of the Queen's accession on 6 February 1952 was commemorated in church services throughout that month. The Queen spent the anniversary weekend at Windsor with her family and the full jubilee celebrations began in the summer of 1977. On 4 May at the Palace of Westminster both Houses of Parliament presented loyal addresses to the Queen, who in her reply stressed that the keynote of the jubilee was to be the unity of the nation. During the summer months the Queen embarked on a large-scale tour, having decided that she wished to mark her jubilee by meeting as many of her people as possible. No other sovereign had visited so much of Britain in the course of just three months – the six jubilee tours in the UK and Northern Ireland covered thirty-six counties. The home tours began in Glasgow on 17 May, with greater crowds than the city had ever seen before. The tours continued throughout England and Wales – in Lancashire over a million people turned out on one day – before culminating in a visit to Northern Ireland. Here we portray a typical street party in Channel View.

THE BOARD SCHOOL

A BEAUTIFULLY CONSTRUCTED arch of flags and greenery festoons the Lower Stennack in 1937 for the coronation of George VI. On the left is the Board School and further down directions to a car park and Alma Terrace. On the right is the old Sheaf of Wheat Inn jutting out to narrow the road. The Sheaf of Wheat was a typical pub of its time but had an interesting addition of a central courtyard where at night locals would sing rousing Cornish choruses. Also on the right a sturdy wall contains the Stennack River as it flows to the sea.

ST IVES' GRANITE Board School, in the Stennack, was completed in 1881 and served the town for almost a century until the new infant and junior schools were built at Trenwith. In 1984, when it was proposed to demolish this fine old building, hundreds of locals marched in protest. It continues to serve the community as The Stennack Surgery. *Stennack* is Cornish for 'Tin Place' as, long ago, there were alluvial tin works all the way down the Stennack stream. This view, taken from Parc Avenue, shows the sprawl of much-needed housing, where once the area was farmland.

DELIVERIES

CARRACK DHU, *c.*1915.
This horse-drawn cart reminds us of the days when all deliveries were made in this fashion, either by the use of horses or people with hand carts. Here the Harbour Bakery, run by the Ward family, is making the rounds. Father, Albert Ward, is on the left, Albert Ward, eldest son, in the middle and Thomas Ward, Valerie Hart's father, on the right. This is a timely reminder of how, in those times, all generations of a family pulled their weight to keep the family business going.

ST IVES' MODERN delivery vehicles can be cheerfully decorated too. Matthew Stevens and Son's vans are embellished

with colourful pictures of the harbour and mouth-watering displays of fish. The Stevens family have run this business for generations. This driver will quickly make his deliveries to nearby restaurants as only very short time parking is allowed along the busy Wharf Road.

RUGBY

OVER THE MANY years of rugby football being played in the town of St Ives a great deal of history has been made including producing County, South West and International players from schoolboy honours to full England caps. In the early years they played at Lower Carnstabba and then at Hellesvean, through to the present day at Alexandra Road. They reached the first six Cornwall County Cup finals in a row (1968/74) and had some close shaves against illustrious opponents. For over 100 years rugby has been important to the people of St Ives and indeed, of Cornwall. This 1960s image shows players in typical team pose. *Back row, from left to right:* J. Major, L. Stevens, W. Toman, E. Stevens, R. Lander, B. Penberthy, P. Beard. *Middle row:* Ref 'Chappy' Chapman, S. Hart, J. Passmore, M. Bowler,

M. Newton, J. Davies, B. Bennetts, S. Berriman. *Front row:* E. Johns, E. Hart, A. Bone, H. Oliver, G. Pearce, J. Bailey, H. Stevens. Players of note include Thomas Wedge – *Chicky*. He was the first St Ives rugby player to play for England. He played in 1907 against France and in 1909 against Wales. When he first arrived at Twickenham, the upper-class officials wouldn't let him in because he wore his fisherman's jersey. In 1951 Harry Oliver was Captain of Cornwall and had outstanding trials for England at Leicester and Twickenham. The year 1957 was when Harold Stevens was Captain of Cornwall and had an England Trial.

IN A MUDDY end of season game against Liskeard Looe, St Ives player Max Bodilly kicks the ball. The St Ives team are ahead. The future for St Ives Rugby Club looks very bright. There is the possibility of the clubhouse and the stand being rebuilt and their Junior and Mini section fields seven teams of varying ages from 7 to 17.

CRICKET

CRICKET HAS BEEN played in the town intermittently since the mid-1800s. The *Penzance Journal* of June 1848 reports a match for which H.L. Stevens of Tregenna Castle donated 3 guineas for the purchase of equipment. The following year, it is reported that '30 of the respectable inhabitants' of the town met to form a club. 'St Ives Win Cup for the First Time' is the newspaper heading for this 1937 image of St Ives Cricket Cup. Familiar local names in the team include Freeman and Hosking, C. Walker, C. Bidgood, J. Cocking, Jack Walker and Willy Baumbach. Subsequently, Sergeant Charles Bidgood became a

prisoner of war in 1942 and endured a 700-mile march through Germany in a dash for freedom and home.

THE PRESENT INCARNATION of the club grew out of a friendly side composed of staff at the local secondary modern school. In 1982 the team was boosted by local players and once again entered into the Cornwall Cricket League playing on Saturdays. An evening team plays on Tuesdays in the West Penwith League. The club now also has a healthy youth section. This action photo shows batsman Jan Harper-Miller at the crease executing a shot. St Ives were playing Paul – and lost, having scored 99 all out in 32.1 overs.

HOUSING

THE 1940s INEVITABLY saw St Ives expand considerably with a large council estate erected at Penbeagle. Locals left the small cottages in Downlong to move into larger family homes – with gardens and bathrooms. Indeed, the coming of the Second World War prevented much of Downlong being demolished due to slum clearance plans. This image captures a street party celebrating the coronation of Queen Elizabeth II in 1953.

ST IVES CONTINUES
to expand around the
Higher Stennack. Great
Carbona Close gets
its name from the old
St Ives Consols Mine.
Carbonas were large and
unusual formations
of ore. When all the
ore was worked out
of the Great Carbona,
the resulting cavern had
to be supported with
massive timbers. When
in 1844 a miner's
candle accidentally
set fire to the timbers
in the Great Carbona,
it burned for six
weeks and destroyed
part of the mine.

THE LEACH POTTERY

BERNARD LEACH IS often referred to as 'the father of modern studio pottery'. Born in Hong Kong in 1887, he studied at the Slade School of Art under Henry Tonks and, at the London School of Art, he studied etching under Frank Brangwyn. He then travelled to Japan and China to study pottery. In 1920 he returned to England to set up the Leach Pottery and, with his colleague Shoji Hamada, he opened a pottery on the outskirts of St Ives. His beautiful domestic stoneware and porcelain soon won international acclaim and many thousands of visitors and students have called at the Pottery to study the techniques used. He was awarded the CBE in 1962. This image shows Bernard Leach and Shoji Hamada loading the kiln.

THE LEACH POTTERY is amongst the most respected and influential studio potteries in the world. Potters Ella Phillips and Britta Wengelar check the results of the latest firing from the old kiln of the 1920s. Scores of potters, students and apprentices from across the world have come to the Leach Pottery to train, creating a uniquely international environment in the heart of Cornwall. Today the newly restored Leach Pottery studio, museum and gallery are continuing the development of Bernard Leach's historic legacy.

MINES

THE MINES OF St Ives from Rosewall Hill. This extraordinary nineteenth-century photograph shows the extent of the mines that once dominated the upper part of the town. In the foreground are the whim (winding) and pumping engine houses of Rosewall Hill and Ransom United Mine, while in the Stennack Valley lie those of the celebrated St Ives Consols Mine. The St Ives Consols Mine was one of the really great mines of the St Ives district. St Ives Consols lies to the west of the town in the upper part of the Stennack Valley, its setts being bounded on the west by Rosewall Hill and Ransom United, and on the east by Wheal Trenwith. The most remarkable feature were its carbonas, the extraordinary deposits of tin found only here and in a few other neighbouring mines. It might be timely to consider the miners who worked in often cramped levels (tunnels) and stopes (galleries) where temperatures would often soar. The depths of

mines in Cornwall were sometimes as much as 300-600m (around 1,000 to 2,000ft) and high temperatures made working conditions in some of the deepest mines appalling. In one local mine, the temperature sometimes soared to above 100°F and in 1884 the east end of the level had to be left to cool for two months before it was possible to work there again.

THE OLD MINE stacks still dominate Rosewall Hill. How the town has grown. In the centre is Consols. On the hillside on the right are the white houses of Penbeagle. In the distance is the Island surmounted by St Nicholas' Chapel and the Coastwatch lookout. Happily much farmland still exists.

TITLES ALSO PUBLISHED
BY ST IVES ARCHIVE

A St Ives Harbour Alphabet by John McWilliams

Breton Fishermen in Cornwall & Scilly: A Century of Friendship by John McWilliams

Changing Times in Old St Ives Vol.1 by Mary Quick

Changing Times in Old St Ives Vol.2 by Mary Quick

Changing Times in Old St Ives Vol.3 by Mary Quick

Changing Times in Old St Ives Vol.4 by Mary Quick

Christmas Tales by Mary Quick

Dear Miss Brooks by Edward Lever

From the Pages of a Lelant Maltsters Pocket Book by John Sell

Lifeboat Gallantry' by Edward Lever

Maritime St Ives by John McWilliams

Memories of Wartime St Ives by Edward Lever & Nigel Jeyes

Memories of People Evacuated to St Ives During World War II by Janet Harris

Memories of Evacuees to St Ives During World War II, Book 2, by Janet Harris

The American 29th Division and St Ives by Edward Lever

The Little Big Book of Seaside Holidays by Mary Quick

The St Ives War Memorial Register of Names by Edward Lever

The St Ives War Memorial Register of Names for The Great War, 1914–1918. Part One: A–J by Edward Lever

The St Ives War Memorial Register of Names for The Great War, 1914–1918. Part Two: K–Z by Edward Lever

The St Ives War Memorial Register of Names for World War 2, 1939–1945. Part One: A–J by Edward Lever

The St Ives War Memorial Register of Names for World War 2, 1339–1945. Part Two: K–Z by Edward Lever

Veterans Remember by Edward Lever